Start with the Trouble

Start with the Trouble

Poems by Daniel Donaghy

The University of Arkansas Press
FAYETTEVILLE • 2009

Copyright © 2009 by The University of Arkansas Press
Manufactured in the United States of America

Text design by Ellen Beeler

⊛ The paper used in this publication meets the minimum requirements
of the American National Standard for Permanence of Paper for Printed
Library Materials Z39.48—84.

Library of Congress Cataloging-in-Publication Data

Donaghy, Daniel
  Start with the trouble : poems / by Daniel Donaghy.
    p. cm.
  ISBN 978-1-55728-907-0 (pbk. : alk. paper)
  I. Title.
  PS3604.O53S73 2009
  811'.6—dc22

                                                    2009018509

for Karen, Abigail, and Eliza
and for my sister, Anne Marie Beecher

Acknowledgments

I offer grateful acknowledgement to the editors of the following publications in which these poems originally appeared: "Burglar," *Broken Bridge Review;* "Still Life with Air Conditioner," *Comstock Review;* "Bruce Springsteen at Aeaea," "Grinding Stone at Sand Creek," and "Tug of War," *Connecticut Review;* "Stadium Traffic," *Desperate Act;* "Landscape with Bikers," *The Dos Passos Review;* "Bottle to Throttle, or After Reading about the Drunk Astronauts, I Recall My Uncle Joe Driving Me to School on Friday Mornings," *Flint Hills Review;* "Hope," "The Medicine of Immortality," "My Mother in Connecticut," "The Spirit of the Promise," and "Start with the Trouble," *Image;* "The Parking Lot," *The MacGuffin;* "The Car" and "Rabbit," *Margie;* "The Loop," *Many Mountains Moving;* "Cold," *New Letters;* "Touch," *Nimrod;* "Abigail's Sandals," *Paterson Literary Review;* "Rally," *Poetry Daily;* "Abigail's Birthday Party" and "Why I Quit," *Prairie Schooner;* "Rooftop," *River Styx;* "For a Poet Missing and Presumed Dead," *South Carolina Review;* "Laertes and the Sandwiches," *Southern Humanities Review;* "The Birth-Control Lesson" and "Rally," *Sou'wester;* "Walt," *Stone Canoe;* "My Father's Patron Saints," *The Sun;* "Baby Tunes," *The Texas Review;* "The Kiss" and "Walking to First Grade," *Zone 3.* "Laertes and the Sandwiches" won the Theodore Christian Hoepfner Award from the *Southern Humanities Review.*

I would like to thank Harry Humes, Steve Myers, Christopher Torockio, and Bruce Weigl, great friends and great writers, who read earlier drafts of this manuscript and offered valuable advice. I would also like to thank the Connecticut State University System for CSU-AAUP research grants that allowed me the time and resources to complete this book.

Special thanks to Karen Donaghy for her constant support.

Finally, I would like to thank Enid Shomer for believing in this book and for her terrific editorial suggestions.

Contents

Start with the Trouble

Stadium Traffic

You're on your way home
when a thousand cars
pour onto Broad Street:
the ball game's over.
No one's going anywhere soon.
It's mid-July: eighty and humid.
You smell like all the crappies in the Delaware,
wear the ache of dock crates in your back.
Your buddy lost two fingers tonight
to a jigsaw: boss said go home early,
stay late tomorrow night.
These people don't appreciate
what they have: time to go to ball games.
You get out among blaring horns
and hustlers hawking T-shirts,
walk the yellow lines like a tight rope,
arms out for balance,
all the way to the corner and back.
Broad Street still as a parking lot,
wound tight as a fist.
You pop the trunk, fish a beer
from your cooler, and pound it.
Back in your car, the radio's
recapping the game:
your team pulled one out
they would have blown last year.
You've blown the last year working
nights while your lady works days.

Night work means bad lighting,
and you've had enough close calls.
You've had enough overtime.
You've had enough.
Something has to give.
Somewhere in the distance a dog
is barking, a husband is coming home.

Tug of War

1.
First time I saw Frankie
two older kids we called

Chickenhead and Froggie
held him by his ankles

off the roof of Perlstein's Glass.
They'd followed Frankie

up a drain pipe
when he fetched a home run ball.

They thought it was funny.
They spat at mothers

who screamed up at them
and laughed at old men

and the rest of us
who waited in the middle

of Sergeant Street
for someone to make them stop.

2.
It was the day after Halloween,
All Saints' Day. The leaves

on the few trees were gone
with the birds except pigeons

like the ones that circled Frankie
as he hung headfirst, screaming.

3.
Frankie, twelve, wanted his mother.
When he yelled for someone

to get her from Tinney's Bar
where she worked,

everyone started yelling it.
When you don't know

what to do, you do
the first thing someone says

that makes sense
or you do nothing.

4.
We heard Frankie's mother
before we saw her,

one long scream after another
until she was under him,

calling *Frankie* and reaching
her hands up as if to pluck him

while she growled
through clenched teeth

at Chickenhead and Froggie
Pull him back up or I'll kill you.

5.
This was a joke gone too far,
a thread woven into all of us

by boys who seemed good
for nothing but scaring people,

a thread they pushed through
fistfights and hard stares,

through rags they soaked
with paint thinner and huffed.

Their lives circled the air
over the closed rug mills,

their futures empty
as their hands

when they pulled Frankie up,
hang jumped to the ground,

then tore down an alley,
laughing, and away.

Still Life with Air Conditioner

Some Saturday before school let out
my father tick-tick-ticked with news radio
and beer around that tiny kitchen,
shooing flies, in minutes
setting the air conditioner in place,
tucking the insulation around
and bringing down the window,
splaying his fingers before the vent
until the air began to chill.

Outside, stray cats, flea bitten and hungry,
mewed block to block for homes.
A shade between orange and brown
blistered along the El's steel girders.
Hydrant flow and halfies.
LL Cool J calling from trunk speakers.
Inside, my mother and a tall glass of water,
cool air against her neck's dried sweat.

The Birth-Control Lesson

Toward the end of sophomore year,
in health class, Miss Applegate spread
    birth-control devices across a table,

    centuries of them, the first spermicide
of alligator dung and honey, sea sponges
    soaked in alcohol and iodine,

    mercury beads Chinese women
swallowed to poison fetuses.
    She picked them up as casually

    as car keys, looked us in the eyes
while she said *penis* and *vagina,*
    semen and *testes* and *breasts,*

    told us premicroscope scientists assumed
that sperm contained tiny people
    and that women were simply incubators,

    told us pulling out didn't always work—
she called it that, *pulling out*—
    told us boys how fast our sperm swam,

    told the girls *What gets in, stays in, ladies,*
that jumping up and down would not
    help, despite what they'd heard.

One in four of you will drop out,
she said, *because you didn't listen.*
    Billy Cook, who talked his girlfriend

    into an abortion, laughed to himself.
Betsy Medina, five months along, stared
    at the clock, while all that talk,

    forgive me, made me cup
Gina Taylor's breast again on her mother's
    flowered couch, made me roll

    her nipples between my fingers,
a softness I carried through nights of shouts
    from the dark kitchen, a scent

    I breathed in while the El sparked
past my bedroom window, convinced
    my life would get no better,

    while whores worked across
the four-lane avenue, sucking and fucking
    strangers in parked cars,

    then throwing filled condoms
onto the street we played on, same wrappers
    as the ones Miss Applegate

    dumped onto her desk that morning—
assorted colors and flavors and scents,
    thin and ribbed, glow in the dark—

Miss Applegate telling us
she would turn her back
        so we could take what we needed,

        all of us shy until someone
snatched a handful, then someone else,
        and they were gone. When word

        spread, so was she, but still
we remember her stories, how Casanova
        gave his mistresses half lemons,

        how the peels blocked his sperm
and the juice killed it, how early condoms
        were called overcoats, how she told us

        that we stood on the brink of greatness
or ruin—*Which will it be?*—and that
        everything was fair game on the test.

The Kiss

Twenty years later
I still see Katie Hickerson
holding out her hand

under our grammar school's
dim basement lights
the night of the spring dance,

bright red feathered hair,
black sequined dress,
green eyes staring up

with what I now see was love.
We were in fifth grade.
By sixth she'd be in Arkansas.

Kids fled the dance floor
when a slow song came on,
so at first it was just Katie and I

for what was not so much
a dance as a dizzy swaying,
her hands around my neck,

my fingertips brushing
the warm small of her back
the way I'd seen in movies.

I don't know what we said
or who danced around us,
or if that song led into another,

or how we slipped away
from each other and back
to our teasing friends.

I know only that the dance
went on for a long time
and that I wanted it to,

and that our heavy feet
barely lifted off the floor,
barely even moved.

I know she had shiny braces
with red rubber bands
and big freckles on her cheeks

and that in another time
I would have given her
the kiss she was waiting for.

Start with the Trouble

Huge hunks of the silver maple
we toppled killing the grass,
trunk pieces split into quarters
a good hundred pounds each,
and my father sighing over my shoulder
as I load the wheelbarrow
like he did those nights
of geometry and physics,
telling me *Start with the trouble,*
get through the toughest part first,

advice I breathe in as I bend my knees
and back, advice I used after he left
and I fought men twice my age—
one who broke into my mother's car,
another who threatened my sister—
always a fight in front of me and two more
waiting with men whose lives would always
be like this, or worse,

                    and me running
after them with bats sometimes, taking out
legs and arms in the middle of a city street
few cops rode down, always shaking as I did it,
never able drive the bat down and through,
never able to roll someone over on his back
and rip the corners of his mouth like a mask,

and because of that I was always afraid
in that El-dark neighborhood, knowing even
when I knocked a man down he would
either rise again like the movie dead
or be replaced by someone else.

Start with the trouble, I'd hear him say,
as if even he believed there was a clear line
between trouble and no trouble,
as if there were a corner I could turn
and slip shadowlessly away from shouts
and whores, burned-out buildings and cars,
graffiti on storefronts and schools,
from the boys we called huffers
who poured paint thinner
into rags they held to their faces,
the friends beaten into stuttered words and steps,
others in jail for twenty or thirty years,
still others killed on the street
while buses passed and kids shot hoops,

as if he could ever find his way
through the trouble he carried silently
in lunchbox and cigarettes, to a place
where he could rise from his hunch
at the kitchen table to laugh and play catch,
to be with us at the end of trouble,
where we might sometimes hold each other,
where we might live in a house
with no roaches and far from other houses
set against each other like rotten teeth,
where the phone would ring

with voices just wanting to say hello,
where music would play and we would sing,
where my parents would dance,
put us to bed early, and have the evening
with each other, then the next evening,
where the car would always start
no matter how much snow piled up,
where we would hang pictures
from Jersey Shore vacations,
where we would walk into the yard
on summer afternoons and shake our heads
at all of our trouble at the start of things,
where I'd feel his arm around my shoulder,
see the other around my sister's,
hear him say again *Start with the trouble,*
you hear me? Make it through that,
mark my words, and you'll be home free.

Grinding Stone at Sand Creek

Kiowa County, Colorado, 1864

Here's a stone she called a mano.
Here's where she wore it flat
grinding corn against rocks
she called metates. Gone the metates,
her wrists of rope and bone beads,
her name, her children's names,
their dreams. Here's Pike's Peak
and its promises of gold.
Gone the treaties and

Chief Black Kettle
Chief White Antelope
Chief Yellow Wolf
Chief Bear Tongue.

Gone creekside screams
beyond a tipi's white flag
and Lincoln's American flag,
which they thought meant peace.
Gone the flag and the child
who hid within his mother's skirt and fell
to howitzers. Gone the howitzers
and the smoke that rose from them
and the mist that clung to prayers.

Gone Colonel John Chivington
and his cause of *Indian extinction,*
his clergyman's collar,
his words to the garrison—
I want victory, not prisoners.

Gone boots that stomped the dead,
hands that sliced back scalps.
Gone with the current the water
that washed them clean,
the rain that finally came
and scattered flies and crows,
that fell across the pocked skin
of cheekbones stretched
like cornmeal over rock
as it lay drying in the sun.

Pieta

At the replica museum,
Sister made us pray the rosary
as Jesus lay in Mary's lap
the way he had as a child—
eyes nearly closed,
gleaming head thrown back—
Mary's outstretched left hand
an invitation into her grief.
But what had that pose
to do with me that empty
gray day of my twelfth year?

Years later, on Sergeant Street
in the rain, I saw the pose again.
There was a fight, someone said.
A lot of shouting, then a knife.
By the time I'd followed
the sirens, it was over:
Mikey from my grade-school class—
skinny Mikey, always-stoned Mikey,
twenty-two years old—lay
across his father's lap.

Mikey's dad was a good man
with a plumbing business
and a stool reserved in Felix's.
He held Mikey's head
in his lap, rocked him like a baby

until the ambulance showed,
whispering *Don't die Mikey don't die.*
He did not hold out his hand, though.
Not the whole time they lay
like that. Not the rest of that night.
Not in the years afterward
until rumors swirled of where he went.

Cold

Because I didn't want my father to die,
I asked him to cut back
on the cheese steaks that clogged
his heart, to quit the smokes
that made him choke and hawk
green phlegm into the sink.
I wanted him to stop drinking
so I wouldn't come home to him
on the cold kitchen floor,
pocked face bloated, broken
brown glass everywhere.
But he'd become a half-listener,
looking up sometimes as if to start
rattling off his life again—
parents dead before he was fourteen,
first wife pregnant by some Italian
while he killed sixteen Koreans—
his bloodshot eyes wet as the night
he dipped my fingers into the shrapnel
wounds in his neck, told me *Shut up
and be grateful for your life.
Now go on, get to bed,* smacking
my ass the way he smacked
my mother's face so many times,
raising that ready hand
when I looked back.

Laertes and the Sandwiches

Near his end my father
takes to making sandwiches,
laying out slices of rye
on the Formica counter,
spreading Dijon mustard,
piling imported ham
and thick Muenster,
pickle slices, and finally
horseradish, homemade,
while the rest of us watch TV.
He shoos away our help,
wanting to be in there alone
with his news radio
under the nicotine-yellow light,
cat or dog rubbing his feet.

When they're ready,
he'll call us to our spots
at the round glass table
while he stands near the sink,
gripping the counter's edge
to keep his balance,
half his weight gone,
no color in his face,
skin pulled skeleton-tight.
What do you think, he'll ask,
meaning the horseradish,
then *Who needs a drink?*

or *How about some chips?*
shuffling over the linoleum
slower than when he drank.

Wasted by years
and unfiltered Pall Malls,
bowed by debt and grief,
he treats us as Laertes
would strangers from Crete,
giving gifts, but never himself.
What test need we pass,
what childhood scar reveal
before he lets us near him,
ex-soldier, ex-con,
before we're left like Odysseus
to flail ragged air
after he's gone?

For a Poet Missing and Presumed Dead

You and your soft, sheltered life
Just go on and on
For nobody special from your world is gone
Just another day
Just another death
Just another Hastings Street whore sentenced to death.

—from the journal of Sarah de Vries, a prostitute missing since
1998 and presumed dead in Vancouver, written in memory of
a friend who had recently disappeared

She was always writing poetry,
her friends said later. They'd tease
the way she stared off
past brake squeak and honking horn

for just the right word,
bruises on her face and hands,
sometimes blood,
and they'd just walk away

when she was really into it,
reading half-finished poems
aloud as if fighting with herself
or the judge who took her kids,

with her father for dying,
her mother for not looking harder

after she ran away at twelve
and fell into seventeen years

of dark alleys in dark cars,
of hepatitis C and AIDS,
of a trash-bag dresser she kept
under the sink in the rented room

she shared with six other women
above an empty pool hall,
where at first light sometimes
she'd read a new poem

like the one about her friend
two weeks gone, the one
she worked on all night,
they said, like she was trying

to keep the friend alive—
that cackle laugh, those mother hugs,
those eyes blue as the Caribbean.
After every job she added something,

they said, another image or line,
another flash of light on shadows
that would soon, like them, like smoke,
disappear into the Vancouver sky.

She was so proud of that one,
they said, and after she read it
aloud, they took turns reading it,
took turns getting each other high.

On the cover of the book
she'd drawn a woman in a white gown,
a smiling sun streaming teardrops.
She had nice things once, they said:

jewelry, clothes. She'd made a lot
of money every night and was pretty.
You'd say she was, too, if you saw
the picture they posted online,

even though it looks like a mug shot,
top lip fat as a slug and bleeding,
left cheek stitched like a rail,
those eyes fixed beyond you

like you're any other curbside john,
like that camera was a waiting car
she'd rather let crush her
than have to face.

My Father's Patron Saints

Athletes for Jesus
is what Sister called them,

writing their birth years
and death years on the board,

passing around pastel portraits
of those holy stoics looking skyward

while arrows impaled them
or lions ripped them apart.

Like athletes keep in shape,
she said, *martyrs stayed ready to die,*

pacing the green tiled rows
those fill-in-the-blank mornings

while we wrote in our best cursive,
Cecelia, patroness of musicians,

Barbara, of prisoners.
And I whispered my own words

to Joachim, patron of fathers,
and Peregrine, of cancer patients,

believing, as I still sometimes do,
that someone could hear me,

staring into my desk's pencil groove
until the room blurred

when I thought of my father,
who on his few good days

could watch a movie with us,
and on his many bad groaned

and hallucinated, crying
one midnight for me, thirteen

and patron of nothing,
to get him a Frosty from Wendy's.

I drove off without much practice
with Christopher on the dash,

slipping up and down
those ten miles without a hitch,

stopping perfectly at lights,
gliding around corners before

I parked outside our row house
and walked into the dark parlor,

where my father lay propped up
by pillows on a rented bed,

lips blistered, kidneys shutting down,
holding out his long fingers

as I crossed the windows' light
to set that cold cup in his hands.

Landscape with Bikers

Lehigh Avenue: traffic backs up
as far as you can see. Rescue lights
spear staccato flashes of blue
and red across the intersection
where a biker and his girlfriend
hit a patch of coal dust, then
a moving truck. The man's right arm
tore from its socket like a doll's.
Blacktop grated the woman's face
down to blood and blond hair
before she hit the truck's tire headfirst.
Sirens scream blocks away.
Neighbors scream and hold each other
and stare like stunned dogs
at bent steel and pooled gasoline
and EMTs who know exactly
how much time they have
before time doesn't matter anymore.

Walt

Reeking of stale Luckies,
Walt came out each night to watch us
play ball in the street, transistor radio

in his lap, brown quart of Ortlieb's,
his legs useless as long as we knew him.
He kept a pull-out bed by the window

and piss jugs beside each chair, so,
he said, he'd only have to *hike the stairs
to shit,* his arms thick as tree trunks

lifting him one half-step at a time,
lowering him the same way
until he crawled back onto his stoop.

Some days he'd fall out the door
flush on his forehead,
cuts still fresh when he waved me

over to dump his piss for a buck,
whispering *I can't reach the sink, babe.
It'll spill over everything,*

then holding out a handful of change
with *Thanks, babe, I owe you,*
before I could tell him no.

The Medicine of Immortality

was what our nuns called it,
the bread of angels, the Lord's supper
on the eve of His pure and holy sacrifice,
their black habits hovering over us

like threats, always the rosary
dangling from a curveless hip,
always chalk dust swirled
on the cracked blackboard,

above which the patron saints
sat awaiting our prayers
and Christ hung forever on the cross,
His body the *viaticum*

that would lift us from that city
toward a *perfect union with God*
once our souls were freed
from their puny earthly shells,

but only if we followed the rules,
all the steps laid out
like hopscotch squares for us
to jump from and to,

salvation another boring chore
like homework, dishwashing,
or sweeping the hall stairs,
Communion's *great and holy moment*

not much more to most of us
than a sure sign that Mass
was almost over, our Sunday
afternoons about to open like gifts

set for an hour on a table
before they're finally given,
our bodies about to slam
each other's until someone cried

during soccer or football games,
our teeth slowly grinding
Christ's unleavened body
until our tongues could fold it

in half, then in half again,
the sum and summary of our faith
going down tougher than broccoli,
the aftertaste of wet paper

tightening our throats
all through the recessional hymn,
which we sang from the diaphragm,
loud as we could, to praise the Lord.

The Parking Lot

Night of the blizzard they're huddled
by a barrel fire when a horn blares,
squad-car cop stares, nails them with his light.
He yells *Go home,* but no one moves.
He yells *Get home. You'll freeze to death,*
but they are home, so they turn away
and toast their hands over the fire,
swing the fifth of JD Black back and forth.
Cop says *Freeze, what do I care?*
slides toward the Front Street action,
red and blue lights spinning.
Bobby's head is spinning,
the fire's dying, and there's no more wood,
so Frankie tells him *Get more wood*
and Bobby says *Where?*
Frankie says *Just get some damn wood*
and Bobby says *Get it yourself*
and expects Frankie to whack him,
so he pulls Candy to his chest,
rests his chin on her frozen hair
while Frankie stomps off to rip
cracked branches from a tree.
Candy stares up and says *I'm cold.*
She gives Bobby those eyes,
sighs *Daddy I'm freezing, please warm me up,*
and shoves her bare hands down her pants.

Bruce Springsteen at Aeaea

"Circe, come out tonight!" he might have said.

It was just another shore gig
between Atlantic City and the Underworld,

another Saturday with a red sun
crouching behind a wine-dark sea

while maidens pushed toward the lip
of the stage like waves,

their hands outstretched
when he reached down, smiling,

part Apollo, part Zeus, part Hephaestus
who made metal sing the songs

of their history and their hearts,
who looked past them to the horizon,

where tomorrow Dawn would rise
from the couch of her reclining

while he and the band were halfway
between Barcelona and Detroit.

He shouted *Is anybody alive out there?*,
part preacher, part huckster,

and when he put a hand to his ear
as he did every night, he heard

more than the living shout back.
From a window beyond the trees

a sorceress watched, potioned
finger curled at her lips.

From the beach, a gray-eyed goddess
matched his every word with her own.

With smoke, light, and dark
Springsteen shifted the shape of things,

rolling out a slow one for Aeolus,
a rocker for Poseidon, pulling

three out-of-town sisters onstage
during an encore and spinning them

one by one into stories
they'd tell the rest of their lives

before he vanished as quickly as he came,
leaving them to sidestep alone

the swine someone wanted once
at the start of their long walk home.

Touch

Another Sunday and up I go again
for the host, hands folded at my belt,
head down before the cross

and the five marks of Christ
the way I learned thirty years ago,
now just as then looking around

to see who's staying behind—
high schoolers, fathers with babies—
the lot dull as any Wal-Mart Tuesday

until a woman my age slides back
to let a family pass, ears glittering,
blue jeans awash in stained light

like Linda Olezcjeck's blue jumper
those eighth-grade, girls-in-one-row,
boys-in-another First Friday Masses,

Linda's mouth closed through every
hymn and prayer, Linda's hair
wing-crisp from strawberry mousse

that wafted like incense
all the way down our pew
to the purgatory of our adolescence.

Lord I am not worthy, we said
after we shook our neighbors' hands,
Frankie Wnek licking his palm

before he squeezed our knuckles,
Joey Reynolds tickling the girls
with his middle finger, all of us

with butterflies in our stomachs
those awkward moments
we touched each other

in the days before we'd sit alone
aching to be touched,
Johnny Wurtzel looking for a hand

to pull him back from heroin,
Angel Beach reaching out
for the fathers of her five kids,

Danny Boyer wanting someone
to do something other than tease
his lisp and his weight, finding

only a .22 he pressed to his head
one night on Snake Road in the rain.
Joseph McCook and his dead mom,

me and my long-gone father,
so many of us, so many empty hands.
And as I fold and fold again

Christ's body with my tongue,
I look up for the woman
who sent me back to Linda

and the rest, but she's gone
as surely as they are
into whatever they've made

of their lives. Back at the pew
I close my eyes and listen
to myself breathing, a prayer

my Buddhist friend taught me.
I feel the air fill my lungs,
sweep through my chest,

shoulders, arms, fingers,
down my legs to my toes,
feel it fill me until I'm nothing

but air and a softened wafer,
familiar taste of boyhood
that I once again swallow down.

Rooftop

When her father left for a long haul
and wouldn't be back for weeks,
we'd sneak onto the third-floor roof
that linked our family's houses.

I was thirteen, she three years older,
the summer she invited me
into the world of my becoming,
corner boys laughing or fighting

beneath us, downtown Philadelphia
all in lights across the horizon
of houses we swore someday
we'd move far away from.

Her parents fought all the time.
Mine had already split up,
and maybe it was something
scared she saw inside of me

that she felt within herself
that led her one evening
to hold the back of my head
and whisper the word *love*.

I'd go inside those nights
and write on a calendar

how many times we kissed
and how often she said that

to me, and I to her.
We would not be out there
on a day like today, first snow
of December, the few leaves

brown and flapping in the wind,
and I don't know what use
she has in my life now
with my daughter

and wife and our house
up in the woods,
but she's here again today
with her black feathered hair

and the crushed velour shorts
all the girls wore then.
It's months before she moved
with her mom into an apartment

across the city and we lost touch.
It's a year or so before
I heard about her baby—
Christopher, his name was—

and about her quitting school,
and nothing else, then or ever,
any trace of her gone with the cars
that raced up and down our avenue,

and with the El trains, the rain,
the light and the dark,
the way I held her to my chest,
the secrets I promised to keep.

Baby Tunes

I've been singing these nights
into my wife's belly,
riffs of nursery rhymes,

country tunes, lullabies,
her belly button the microphone,
her uterus the crowd,

her heart the drum machine
giving away my lack of rhythm
through "Kum Ba Ya"

and "Greensleeves,"
"Can You Count the Stars,"
nothing coming back whole

until tonight and the songs
I grew up on, so fitting now:
"Baby, I Love You" popping

into my head, and suddenly
I'm nothing but baby tunes, baby:
I'm Sweet Baby James,

I'm the jukebox at Martin's Deli,
I'm the record player
my cousin Joey spun hits on

while our fathers drank beer,
I'm Woody Guthrie crooning
"Curly Headed Baby"

outside a Columbus stockade,
I'm Janis howling "Cry Baby"
on a deserted California beach,

I'm the Righteous Brothers,
Carl Perkins, Marvin Gaye,
sure I could go on all night,

"Boogie Woogie Baby,"
"Baby, You Can Drive My Car,"
our baby six months along

turning toward my stops and starts,
tapping her brand new foot
in the place where time begins.

Why I Quit

So the son gets a D and the mother calls
to say I might as well have shot him in the head

because Dartmouth won't take him now
and clearly I don't know what's at stake.

The kid's a B student on his best day—
can't tell Shakespeare from Seamus Heaney—

but she's talking Dartmouth because
her husband's father invented the flip-top can

or some such thing and she thinks
she's got something coming for that.

This is private school, after all,
and if I hold the wrong kid accountable,

I could be shucking pizzas on nights
and weekends beside kids smart enough

for my school but too poor to get in.
Flour, tomato sauce, pepperoni, yeast—

these are what I think about
while the mother tells me her son's stool

is bloody from the stress I've caused
and that she'd be calling the school's Head

to rescind the check for the new library.
Rest assured, she says, *your name will come up.*

I put her on speakerphone,
stretch out my arms like scales

to weigh the odds he'll choose me
over a fat donation. I see the future:

a ribbon cutting, the patter of applause,
a breathy speech about giving

our fine future leaders
the chance to get all they deserve.

I feel my skin soaking in kitchen grease
like back in high school, when I stood for hours

wondering how a pizza could fly like that—
off the thumbs and back to the thumbs—

stretching without tearing in skilled hands,
a marvel one must step back to enjoy,

like the seams of stitches you'd need
after running through a sliding glass door,

or a metal splinter burrowed into your palm,
or this mother, still talking when I hang up.

The Car

I'm trying to open a frozen trunk in December,
pulling on the lip above the license plate
until the car starts bouncing, until I'm thirteen
again with a Dodge Dart's bumper in my hands,
standing shoulder to shoulder with the men

of my neighborhood trying to lift a car
off my friend Teddy, who ran into the street
after his football. Teddy didn't have time
to jump out of the way or hold out his hands
or yell *Stop*. What he did, it's taken me

twenty years to remember: he lay down
in the middle of Jasper Street and tried to duck.
He curled around his football just before
half the car thumped over him. One minute
he was the Eagles quarterback

and I their best receiver. The next
there was a quick pool of blood
and no one around except the driver,
an old woman, who shook splayed fingers
in front of her face. Behind closed windows,

she tried twice to back up
before cutting the engine. I took off
for the closest adults, the ten or so dads
in Tinney's Bar, who rushed like cops
onto the street they sang and fought on

almost every night. Ray Dangler helped
the woman to a stoop. Eddie Dillaplane
shuffled home for his bumper jack.
Big Joe Russell and the other dads and I
each found a spot on that bumper,

counted to three, and tried to lift.
Teddy's dying, someone said. *His eyes are open,
but they're all white. Oh my God.*
We counted and lifted, counted and lifted,
but couldn't get the wheels off the ground.

I looked under the car and breathed in
the muffler's oven-heat, saw
Teddy's right leg twisted completely around.
The rest I saw from the sidewalk.
Firemen took over. My mother pulled my back

to her chest and hugged my arms.
People moved so often then.
Within a year, Teddy was gone with his mom
and his crutches to somewhere in California,
where his mom had a friend.

Half a life later, under constellations
we didn't know about in smog-dim Philadelphia,
I pour warm water along the trunk's edges
and lift again—three, four, five times.
At last, the ice cracks. The trunk flies open and free.

Santa and the Sled Dogs

We knew he was close
    when a fire truck crept
onto the main road stately
    as a limousine,

its sirens howling through
    the carolers' medleys,
no snow yet, not too cold,
    the red lights swirling

across houses and trees
    and across the town green,
where kids crowded together
    to give Santa their lists.

Then far-off sleigh bells,
    a hush over the crowd.
Then a fireman's spotlight
    on the sled dogs

pulling Santa into view—
    not a helper,
my daughter says later,
    but the real one—

and who could argue against
    that suit and beard
or that booming voice
    that pushed his pack

past the war memorial
　　and Methodist church?
Who could argue there was any place
　　in that night for doubt

when Santa halted his dogs
　　in front of my daughter,
then bent to say *I remember you.*
　　Have you been good?

I don't need to tell you
　　what she dreamt of
under her dog posters
　　and glow-in-the-dark stars.

Or about my sweet weeks
　　of leverage after Santa
gave me a card with his number
　　and e-mail address

and told me to keep it handy,
　　its frosted edges glistening,
its reindeer's red nose
　　alight at least one more year.

Burglar

I opened the front door to a black coat
crashing into the basement,
work boots thundering down stairs,
then silence that hovered in the kitchen
like a father after money runs out.

We were renting the house,
and I, stupid as that first person dead
in a horror film, followed after him,
thought he was the landlord,
here finally to fix the furnace.

When I reached the bottom step,
a voice told me I was going to die.
From behind the furnace came
eyes wide as the electrocuted
and arms spread like a wrestler's.

In the instant before fear,
I felt sorry for him, shorter
than I thought a burglar
should be, no front teeth,
face pulled under the weight

of years of such living.
Then the how/why questions
that took me back to boyhood,
my father's kitchen-dark words
Hit him before he hits you

making me hurl two hooks
that drew bubbles of blood
and dropped the burglar to a knee.
When he ran up the stairs,
I snatched an iron from a shelf

and tried to throw it through his back.
Even now I love watching
it bend the middle of him forward,
knock out his fight and wind.
I jumped on his back and wrapped

the black cord around his neck.
Neither of us was breathing.
In movies, that's when the cops come,
my wife jumps from a squad car
while the cops cuff the burglar

and read him his Miranda rights,
red and blue lights spinning.
Or else a neighbor comes to help,
knows something about tying knots,
makes the call and all ends well.

Alone, though, I held a man's life
in my hands, if only a taker's life,
if only the life of a burglar
who'd packed bags of our things
and set them like his groceries

by a window, and next to them
a Coke for the way home.

How careful he must have been,
hiding in bushes or behind a car
when we left that morning,

walking like he belonged
toward the window he'd crack
and reach through for the latch.
How cocky he must have been
as he crept from room to room,

filling bags, smoking, spilling
drawers, thinking he had all day.
Now he wanted only to get away—
he told me so with hands and feet
that flailed like he was drowning.

I let up and he tore from me,
his boots slashing and carving
through the mud toward the woods.
The police never found him.
He ran off with only that life.

Abigail's Sandals

Our two-year-old daughter
clomps and totters down the hall
when I come home, calling my name,
thudding twice before finally
making it to the kitchen,
where she stops across the room
to show off her new sandals,
twirling like mom taught her,
saying *Ta-da!*, her latest word,
looking up in a moment
she gives me like a gift,
pointing down at her toes
and the pink and purple flowers,
smiling, one knee scratched,
pulling me out of myself
and that place I've been all day,
pulling me by the hand
back to her bright blue eyes
and jellied sundress
until we're sitting together
in the doorway's stack of shoes,
noses pressed together,
her sticky hands patting my hair,
hands each the size of my palm,
smooth as the ears of the kitten
I had in that other kitchen,
which I held in my room
when my parents yelled

beneath the ceiling fan that wobbled
and threatened to fly off,
my father's hands tightening into fists
to knock my mother down,
my daughter bringing me back
from all that—jumping up, twirling,
looking again at her sandals—
into day after day like this one.

Abigail's Birthday Party

It's our daughter's birthday,
so the yard is festooned
with Pooh hats and plates,
streamers and cups,
tablecloths over old paint.
Her grandparents have driven
upstate with a plastic convertible,
her uncle has flown in
with a blue and yellow house
with its six-tone doorbell
and clock that never moves.
Our daughter still loves Pooh
and his friends, but when
we ask her to name
the blue donkey, the kangaroo
between Rabbit and Piglet,
she'll have none of it.
Today it's the house she wants,
her first taste of freedom—
pink plastic dishes and pots,
rubber green phone she picks up
to call the neighbor's dog
and the giraffe at the zoo.
And of course she wants the car,
in love already with how the yard
unfolds before her like a wish,
her trunk packed full,
steering wheel twirling

past picnic table and pool,
waving goodbye to us
as she skirts the woods' edge,
her car glowing like a fire
because the sun is going down
and the roads she'll take
without us are almost in view.

Rally

A third day of wet gray skies,
a stalled chill pressing on me like a hand

three years after my mother's death
during a blizzard that shut down

my town two hundred miles north,
gray skies unloading

until the airports closed, the roads,
until she ran out of breath

the same day she'd called to tell me
she was all right, wait out the storm,

her voice strong with what doctors
called her *rally to say goodbye,*

common, they see it all the time,
her voice so clear in my head today

I want to answer it, so I do,
with a few words to the empty house

and with her hard life burning
in my stomach when I imagine her

looking out past her walker
to the gray sky outside,

and beyond that to my father,
her parents, the God she'd prayed to

all her life, especially at the end,
those rosary beads still wrapped

around her fingers
when I got there an hour too late.

The Loop

at the Baseball Hall of Fame, Cooperstown, NY

Even here my father's sorry end
returns—his all-of-a-sudden gray
hair and dull eyes, his labored croak-speech
back in my head as I watch The Babe's
farewell looping on a TV screen,
his forced smile, his pursed lips the same
as my father's a decade ago,
Ruth's two-fisted lean into his cane
a sad parody of his raising
that 54-ounce bat like God's hand
in the '32 Series, pointing
to Chicago's bench after the blast
that looked like it might never come down,
which of course it did, just as he did,
ending up a sideshow for the Braves
save one more great day, when three flew out,
the last three he hit, and he shuffled
like his own ghost around the bases.
Maybe you've heard his low, scraping voice
saying goodbye at the Stadium,
or else seen that gait in a parent
as I did when my father pushed through
my wedding day, tie Windsor knotted,
his hands shaking, back slumped like a birch.

In the photograph we're both smiling,
he holding his breath against the pain
as Ruth did in his camel-hair coat
while cameras flashed, waving one last time
to all of his fans, then vanishing
into the ash-gray of that moment.
You can get so far from things you think
you've moved finally moved away from them,
that you've come to the end of the reel
and it won't loop around. That you're free.

Bottle to Throttle, or After Reading about the Drunk Astronauts, I Recall My Uncle Joe Driving Me to School on Friday Mornings

*At least twice recently, astronauts were allowed to fly even
though they had consumed alcohol within the previous twelve
hours, thereby violating the waiting period known among
pilots and astronauts as the "bottle to throttle" rule.*
—Aviation Week and Space Technology, *July 26, 2007.*

Here he is again—not my uncle, really,
my father's best friend—honking at 8 a.m.,
ripping back the tab from his can of Ortlieb's
after the third shift at FedEx, loading freight.
Enough to drive anyone to drink, he says—
a hundred boxes an hour to unload,
forty more to load, not even one smoke break.
This is before the Challenger explodes,
before NASA shuts the program down to check
every rocket booster, every O-ring seal,
these the Cold War Fridays that Uncle Joe has
only his beer, the ride with me, his eight-tracks,
and a one-room apartment on Butler Street
to look forward to before another shift,
his greasy hair slicked into a pompadour,
a silver cross hanging over his T-shirt
while he jerks his blue '61 Thunderbird
from stop sign to stop sign until Route 13,

when he opens all eight cylinders for a
quarter-mile, that 390 engine's G-force
blowing us back against those cracked leather seats,
his right forearm like a bar against my chest
as he crunches that gas pedal to the floor,
his left hand gripping and ungripping the wheel,
his eyes, bloodshot and unblinking, fixed far off
as if he's trying to lift us into flight.

Rabbit

In my sixth summer,
I snapped a rabbit's neck
with my thumbs.

I meant to save him.
He'd squeezed through
the chicken-wire cage

my father made
and hopped to the chain links
that kept us safe

from our neighbor's dogs.
There was no change
between before and after,

no twitch or cry,
just his weight in my hands
and a line of blood

along his throat
that was beyond undoing.
I knew what he was thinking.

He'd have made it through.
But the dogs had their ideas,
too, snapping and drooling

first at me, then at the rabbit.
I wanted to save him,
so I lifted him to my face

and asked like my father
What were you thinking?
I shook him

when he looked back
to the dogs, up on haunches now.
No No No, I said,

bad things could happen.
I kept shaking, I guess.
Blood shone through his eyes.

His fur felt like feathers.
When I finished talking,
I pulled him to my chest.

I wasn't angry at all.
When his head fell back,
a new world opened,

full of blame only for me.
In my room I tried to tape him whole.
I've had thirty years

to think about this.
I didn't mean to kill the rabbit.
I didn't mean to shake so hard.

My Mother in Connecticut

After the snow stops
and the sky opens cloudless
over the mountains, and after
three pairs of cardinals
flutter back to our feeder,
I stand by the kitchen window
watching them as I did
two years ago this week,
talking to you on the phone,
tube in your throat capped,
strength, you said, coming back
to your arms and legs.
Then the snow started again,
and you told me not to drive
the three hundred miles,
that you'd see me Thursday,
when we could walk together
the halls of that awful hospital.
I'll see you Thursday, I kept saying
after you or I said something else,
or after one of that call's many silences
in which I breathed you in
like I do today, until I can see you
out there beneath the spruce,
blue coat collar up,
dog barking and jumping,
your back stooped, left hand
waving me outside. I don't

have to squeeze my eyes today
to hear you whisper my name
or feel your cracked lips on my cheek
when our time ran short.
And I can't keep you from leaving,
as I couldn't that Wednesday night,
your eyes a lighter blue than the sky's,
your permed hair flaked with snow
like the sweetbriar's thin branches.

Walking to First Grade

You asked over pancakes
if we could walk to school
instead of drive, so the trip

that might have taken
a minute takes twenty,
so we get to hold hands

the length of the gravel drive
and all along our road,
your black shoes scratching stones,

hair ponytailed, front tooth
crooked and loose.
Trucks arc around us

past the Christmas tree farm
and Protestant church,
and for no one reason

I think again of my parents
in their early graves,
hear them over me mornings

like this, whispering.
At the school's entrance,
you pan the sea of strangers;

we don't talk much.
We wait by black-eyed Susans
and coneflowers for the doors

to open, and when they do,
I hold you at arm's length,
feeling again my mother's hand

tousle my hair, my father's kiss,
but I don't tell you that.
Kids' sneaks scuffle past us

on the sidewalk, bus gears
strain to a stop. As we walk the hall,
I watch you move away

past the music room and library,
past the cafeteria with its murals
and folded tables, until at last

we're outside of Room 3:
name tags and pencil cases,
friends and strangers,

work stations, job charts.
After a peck on the cheek
I'm alone in the brick hallway,

where from a squat
I watch you shake hands
with your teacher,

turn in your lunch money,
slide off toward your new desk
without looking back.

The Spirit of the Promise

Amazing how the prayers come back,
    the cues to stand and kneel and sit,
the hymns rising after so many years

into the air of this small old church.
    We lean together in summer
sunlight as the priest wafts past

in an incense cloud and the small choir
    sings off-key in corner light.
Yesterday you asked what church was

and who lives there, and for a while
    I felt so bad I could see
all my grade school nuns shaking

their heads at me, all those priests
    putting down their Chesterfields
to tell me how many decades

of the rosary I'd need to say
    to be forgiven for this one,
but most clearly I could see my parents,

who left me little but this God
    they went to their graves
believing in and asking for forgiveness.

I want to tell you how good it felt
        to go back, that I could feel them
beside me in the pews, dressed perfectly

in the clothes my sister and I
        buried them in. I want
to tell you more about them,

about their many years of nights
        slumped in our kitchen,
the only light glowing from the tips

of cigarettes that would kill them.
        But that's for me to carry.
Some words fit best underground.

There will be a time for others.
        Until then, since you
brought it up, *church* is a building,

or a service, or a group of Christians.
        It's also something
you can give, so I'll give it here:

a blessing to a young woman
        at the start of something or,
like you, the start of everything.

Hope

I'm thinking again of Pandora
and the box, of the boy
committed to stopping her

until she undid her golden braids
and got her way.
He'd wanted to open it, too,

but he'd made a promise
to a friend, and for a while
the promise was relevant.

I'm thinking of irrelevance,
of word and spirit and heart,
how the boy leaned against

her warm shoulder for a look
just as the evil Passions swooped
like mosquitoes to their necks,

the hundred and fifty Sorrows
stinging them with guilt and worry
they'd carry all their lives,

the paradise of childhood gone,
work now to be done,
clothes to mend, hunger and thirst

stopping their laughter.
I'm thinking, too,
of my own irrelevance

when friends now dead chopped crank
on hand mirrors and snorted it
through rolled-up dollar bills, when

Wild C, who was like a brother,
jumped in front of an El train
after his girlfriend didn't take him back.

Philadelphia: that city a box of sorrows,
a flock of swirling darknesses.
And don't forget the many Cares

Pandora let loose,
the black clouds that trailed them
like doppelgangers. Follow them

over doorways and skyline.
Listen to them darting about, tickling
before they burrow in and spread.

In a week my daughter will be six.
This summer she's in paradise:
swimming, her cat, books, ice cream.

I'm thinking again of Pandora
because I'm thinking of Hope,
the last force to rise from the box,

the only answer to Troubles
like loneliness and age.
Fear is the knot in a golden cord

twisted around the heart,
without end or beginning.
Hope is the hand that unties it.